Contents

Words shown in **bold** in the text are explained in the glossary.

All the places in this book are shown on the map on page 22.

What Is a Home?

A home is a place to stay cool.

A home is a place to stay dry.

A home is a place to stay warm.

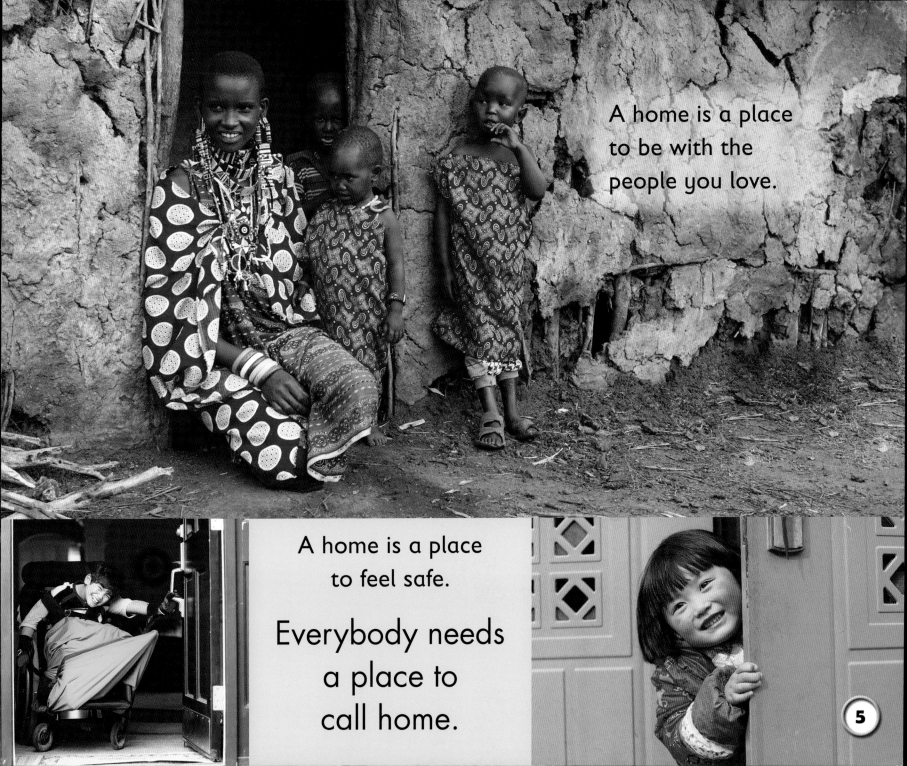

A home is a place
to be with the
people you love.

A home is a place
to feel safe.

Everybody needs
a place to
call home.

5

A Himba Hut

The Himba people of Namibia, in Africa, move from place to place to find grass for their goats and cattle.

Wherever they settle, Himba people build small homes called **huts**.

Milking the goats

A Himba hut

The huts are made of branches covered in dried mud and cow dung.

Once Himba children are about three years old, they leave their parents' hut. Then they share a hut with other children.

A Floating Village

On Tonlé Sap lake in Cambodia people live in floating villages.

There are floating shops, petrol stations and churches.

The children who live here travel to their schools by boat.

A floating school

A floating shop

A floating church

Floating houses

Some families make their homes in houses that float on the water. Others live on houseboats.

A floating garden

Rainbow Homes in the Snow

On the tiny island of Kulusuk, the land turns white in winter.

There's still a rainbow of colours to be seen, however.

That's because everyone on Kulusuk lives in brightly painted wooden houses.

Kulusuk is just off the coast of Greenland.

The island is home to fewer than 300 people.

Lots of sled dogs live on Kulusuk. They pull the sleds that people use to travel over the ice and snow.

Living in a City

Around the world, billions of people live in big cities.

Some people in a city live in houses.

San Francisco in the United States

Many city homes do not have a garden. People spend time outdoors in parks and playgrounds.

Some people live in flats, or apartments, high above the ground.

Apartment blocks in Hong Kong

A Home in a City Slum

Not everybody who lives in a city has a house or flat.

Around the world, millions of very poor people live in parts of cities known as **slums**.

They build small homes from materials they find on the streets and on rubbish dumps.

These boys from a slum in Delhi, in India, are burning rubbish to stay warm.

Slum homes usually have no electricity, toilets or water for drinking, cooking and washing. In Delhi, thousands of families may share just one water tap in a slum area.

A home in a slum in Delhi, India

A House with a Tower

On the Indonesian island of Sumba, people live in small villages.

Each village is made up of houses that have towers on the roofs.

A water buffalo

The people of Sumba are farmers.

They raise pigs, water buffaloes and chickens.

The tower of a Sumba house is used as a safe place to keep precious objects. People believe that the **spirits** of their **ancestors** live in the towers of their homes.

A tower

Animals live in the bottom part of the house.

People live in this part of the house.

A Home on the Move

Many people in Mongolia are **nomads**.

They move from place to place to find fresh grass for their horses, cattle, camels, sheep and goats.

Mongolian nomads live in tent-like homes called *gers*.

A camel carrying a ger

A ger has a wooden frame. The frame is covered with layers of felt made from sheep's wool. It has an outer covering made from waterproof canvas.

These children are watching TV inside their ger.

It takes less than an hour to build or dismantle a ger!

19

A Place to Call Home

Every year, many people have to leave their homes to escape from dangers such as floods, earthquakes or wars.

In 2011 a war began in Syria.

Millions of people became **refugees**.

They left their homes and found safety in camps in Syria and nearby countries.

People in refugee camps often have to live in tents.

Many refugees live in a camp for years.

They hope that one day it will be safe to go home.

Children from Syria at a refugee camp

21

Where in the World?

Canada
Page 4

Kulusuk, Greenland
Pages 10–11

England
Page 12

Syria
Pages 20–21

Mongolia
Pages 18–19

United States
Page 12

China
Page 5

North America

Europe

Asia

Africa

South America

United States
Page 5

Hong Kong, China
Page 13

Australia

India
Pages 14–15

Brazil
Page 4

Senegal
Page 4

Namibia
Pages 6–7

Kenya
Page 5

Cambodia
Pages 8–9

Sumba, Indonesia
Pages 16–17

Glossary

ancestor
A relative who lived a long time ago.
For example, your great-grandparents
and great-great-grandparents are
your ancestors.

hut
A small house that usually has just one
room and one storey.

nomad
A person who regularly moves from one
area to another and does not live in one
place all the time.

refugee
A person who has been forced to leave
his or her home to escape danger and
needs to be protected.

slum
An overcrowded and often dirty area
where many people live in poverty.
A slum is usually in a city or on the
edge of a city.

spirit
An invisible part of a person that many
people believe lives on after death.
For example, a ghost is a type of spirit.

Index

Learn More Online

To learn more about homes
around the world, go to
www.rubytuesdaybooks.com/homes